THE POWER OF
persistence

Sound Wisdom Books by John Martin

*Focus on Today: How Living in the Present
Can Transform Your Future*

*Choose Your Perspective: 7 Tips for High
Performance through Intentional Thinking*

Empower Yourself: 7 Steps to Personal Success

*Increase Your Personal Productivity: Your Guide to
Intentional Living & Doing More of What You Enjoy*

*The Power of Persistence: How to Stop Quitting on
Yourself and Achieve Your Goals: Gain Confidence,
Overcome Failure, and Build Willpower and Ambition*

THE POWER OF
persistence

How to Stop Quitting on Yourself and Achieve Your Goals: Gain Confidence, Overcome Failure, and Build Willpower and Ambition

JOHN MARTIN

Published and Distributed by
SOUND WISDOM
PO Box 310
Shippensburg, PA 17257-0310
717-530-2122
info@soundwisdom.com
www.soundwisdom.com

ISBN 13 TP: 978-1-64095-469-4
ISBN 13 eBook: 978-1-64095-470-0

For Worldwide Distribution, Printed in the USA
1 2 3 4 5 6 / 26 25 24 23

For Nate, thanks for the support.

CONTENTS

"*There is no substitute for persistence! It cannot be supplanted by any other quality!*"

"*Remember this, and it will hearten you in the beginning, when the going may seem difficult and slow.*"

"*Those who have cultivated the habit of persistence seem to enjoy insurance against failure. No matter how many times they are defeated, they finally arrive up toward the top of the ladder.*"

—Napoleon Hill, *Think and Grow Rich*

"Nothing in this world can take the place of persistence. Talent will not; nothing is more common than unsuccessful men with talent. Genius will not; unrewarded genius is almost a proverb. Education will not; the world is full of educated derelicts. Persistence and determination alone are omnipotent."

—Calvin Coolidge

INTRODUCTION

> *"We must have perseverance and above all confidence
> in ourselves. We must believe that we are gifted for
> something and that this thing must be attained."*
>
> —MARIE CURIE

An old familiar story called *The Tortoise and the Hare*, one of the famous fables of Aesop, tells the fate of the cocky hare who makes fun of the slow pace of the tortoise. He asks the tortoise, "Do you ever get anywhere?"

To which the tortoise proceeds to challenge the hare to a race to prove that, yes, he gets places sooner than most would think.

The finish line is agreed upon and the race commences. Naturally, the hare takes a large lead being the faster animal. In order to further humiliate the tortoise and because he figures he has the time, the hare decides to take a short nap along the path of the race. He falls asleep, the tortoise passes him, and everyone learns the moral of the story: "Slow and steady wins the race."

Another takeaway from this story is the power of persistence. The hare was so far in front of him, the tortoise could have reasonably given up and said, *"Ummm…that was a bad idea after all,"* or, *"Wow, I had no idea the hare was that fast."* He didn't know that the hare would foolishly decide to take a nap, but still he kept plodding along even though he clearly was the slower of the two animals.

The tortoise was determined to do his best in this race that he had begun, and the results would be what they would be.

Many of us quit because we are too focused on the results that never seem to happen soon enough—instead of staying the course and *becoming* the type of person who never quits. Instead of becoming, too many people are focused on getting somewhere fast.

You may be thinking of times in your own life when you quit too early—I know I can. There are many cases we don't know about, some external factors that would have propelled us to victory if we would have only kept plodding along, slow and steady, in our efforts to reach our goals.

"Strength does not come from physical capacity. It comes from an indomitable will."—Gandhi

What we do know is that most people do not finish the race and achieve the goals they set for themselves.

In fact, to take the New Year's resolutions that are traditionally made in January as an example, *Forbes* reports that 80 percent of people quit their resolutions by February.[1] Think of all the books half-written, the weight lost and then regained, the exercise regimen temporarily adhered to, the good business ideas with no follow-through. Think of all that could have been if more people stayed true to their "resolutions."

When you think of these truths, it becomes clear that persistence might be one of the most valuable skills you can develop to help you move up, to advance beyond the status quo.

So how do you become persistent when you have historically started many goals and then quit for some reason or another? Is persistence something you can learn?

History shows us that persistence can be practiced and learned by anyone who desires to achieve a goal.

CREATE AN IMAGE

To begin, you must create a clear image in your mind of what it is that you want to achieve. Whether it is an image of you being in good physical shape from a healthy diet and exercise, operating a flourishing social media platform, being a successful business owner, or being in a rewarding relationship, whatever it is you want to accomplish, work on developing a strong, concrete image of this reality in your mind.

Many people quit because they are unsure of what they want.

Once you have a clear idea of the goals you want to accomplish, then you can use your subconscious mind to reinforce these images so that the accomplishments become more real to you.

ESTABLISH GOOD HABITS

Along with using the subconscious to reinforce the positive results of your goals, dreams, and efforts, you will establish habits that help you build persistence.

What habits build persistence? Some you know, others may surprise you. One thing is for sure, if you are willing to work on instilling these daily actions into your journey through life, you will gain the ability to persist in your goals for as long as you want…and you will experience the success you imagine.

This book gives you the motivation and inspiration you need to keep going strong when you want to quit. It can be picked up and opened to any page during moments of self-doubt, self-pity, and discouragement.

The Power of Persistence is meant to be a starting point. Every time you are ready to give up, read a few lines and see what happens. My hope is that you will read something that gives you the strength and courage

> *You will never know if your goal is reachable if you quit now.*

to keep going, if only for another hour. Maybe that hour will turn into a day, a week, a month, and a year!

QUITTING IS NOT AN OPTION

In fact, quitting has often been called the only true failure in life. So to be successful at whatever you want to do, don't quit. Don't let quitting be an option. Choose to persist.

There is tremendous value in developing a character of persistence, and through your efforts to keep going when you want to quit, you gain confidence.

Understanding and remembering that persistence is more important than talent or genius helps you keep working when you doubt yourself.

Persistence leads you to make one more phone call, send one more email, create one more piece of content, and-or do one more exercise.

Persistence is a way of thinking.

Persistence is a way of thinking. And creating a persistent mindset is a great starting point for developing a set of tools to help you keep working when you would have rather stopped for the day. Or for when you are ready to throw in the towel and quit altogether due to some seemingly major setback. These "persistent mindset" tools will help you get up again, and over time, they will strengthen your resolve even more.

In your effort to reach your goals, always remember that tenacity is more valuable than talent. Write this down and put it somewhere you will see it each day: **Tenacity is more valuable than talent!** Remind yourself of this truth every time you start to get down on yourself and think you're not good enough.

Tenacity is more valuable than talent.

You *are* good enough. Once you get your self-talk right and your habits in line with the person who can accomplish what you are after, your life will change.

You *are* strong enough to keep going just for today, and right now that is all that matters—so let's get going!

NOTE

1. Lisa Bodell, "New Year's Resolutions Fail. Do This Instead," *Forbes .com*, December 19, 2022; https://www.forbes.com/sites/lisabodell /2022/12/19/new-years-resolutions-fail-do-this-instead/?sh=4a693 8367c8b; accessed May 9, 2023.

CHAPTER ONE

INSTILL DAILY HABITS THAT CULTIVATE PERSISTENCE

"Habit is persistence in practice."
—OCTAVIA BUTLER

"Persistence is the direct result of habit."
—NAPOLEON HILL

When asked if perseverance can be developed, famous personal development author and speaker Jim Rohn answered, *"Yes, and there are some very powerful techniques that can help you learn it. By far, the most important tool you can use in developing perseverance is a personal list of challenging, realistic, well-defined, and highly-rewarding goals."*

With Rohn's answer in mind, at the end of each chapter of this book, there are prompts and questions for reflection to help you come up with your own list of goals related to the chapter you've just read that you can customize according to your personal vision of what you want to achieve.

YOUR MORNING ROUTINE

Let's start at the beginning.

Your morning routine—begin to establish habits that support your goal of becoming persistent. Every morning, starting tomorrow, build belief and trust in yourself by maintaining a routine that will become a habit. Day one, day two, day three, and so on, take pride in your consistency, not in the results yet. Just keep working on a specific daily program, your morning routine.

Avoid doing anything that holds you back; replace with activities that propel you forward toward reaching your goals. Taking a couple of positive steps each day goes a long way toward creating the future you want.

Start by analyzing your current typical morning routine, say, from the time you wake up to the time you begin to work. Write down the details so you can evaluate them. What time do you wake up? Do you eat breakfast? Drink coffee? Take a shower? Put as many details down as possible.

After you write down your current morning routine, write down what you would call your *ideal* routine including:

- What would you change about your current morning activities?

- What changes in your current routine would buy you more time?

- What might make you feel more energetic and less stressed when you approach your workday?

Write it all down. You can even make a list of pros and cons about your current routine and then figure out how to eliminate the cons.

The goal is to create a morning routine that puts you in the best state of mind to persist throughout what may be the most challenging day possible. When you start off the day by hitting all your goals for the "little" things—like waking up at a certain time and exercising, or journaling and reflecting, or reading, etc.—you are optimizing your chances at perseverance and pushing through obstacles that come up later that day.

Setting yourself up for a successful day begins every morning.

YOUR EVENING ROUTINE

And since the way we feel in the morning is somewhat dependent on what happens at night, think about what you can do to optimize the way you feel when you wake up. For example, it is best *not* to:

- Drink caffeine close to bedtime
- Drink too much alcohol in the evening
- Eat food that is not easily digested before going to sleep
- Exercise close to bedtime

When you lay down in bed at a time that allows for ample hours of rest and sleep, read books or magazines instead of watching videos on your phone or watching TV; keep your room dark.

Try a couple variations of nighttime routines and morning routines to see if you need to make some changes.

This advice may seem simplistic, but when you think about it, it really is. I mean, our life and achievements are simply choices that we make in the moments of the day. Whether we quit or push on for another two minutes are almost always decisions that we make on our own. And often those decisions are based on how we feel.

So work on making yourself feel better. Don't rely on chance.

You don't always naturally feel good. Even if you have a great night of sleep and all your choices are good the day before, you can wake up on the "wrong side of the bed" and be in a bad mood first thing in the morning. That is why it is so important to take control of your mind.

And you can't always just will yourself into thinking positive thoughts or being grateful.

ACTION OVER ATTITUDE

Sometimes, action is a must. Drink water, take deep breaths, and get into some physical activity like a brisk morning walk, calisthenics, or even a resistance workout. Once you become active, it will be impossible to remain in a state of negativity. You will have raised your dopamine levels at least for the time being.

Dopamine is a neurotransmitter, a chemical messenger in the brain that affects movement, motivation, reward, and pleasure. Dopamine is involved in the brain's reward pathway, which controls feelings of pleasure and reinforcement. It is released in response to rewarding stimuli, such as receiving a compliment, achieving a goal, or engaging in pleasurable activities like eating tasty food or engaging in social interactions.

Disruption of dopamine can affect your mental and physical health. For example, conditions like depression and addiction have been linked to changes in dopamine function. So when you use alcohol, drugs or other negative influences to raise your dopamine levels, it has lasting effects that you might not want. Alternatively, exercise and conversation are much healthier ways to raise your dopamine.

There might be days when you have to exercise repeatedly to change a bad mood into a positive mood. That's okay. Exercise is good for you as I'm sure you've heard. When you're active, you naturally raise your level of good vibration to transfer a higher form of energy to yourself and others. This stimulation contributes to your day going much better, even in the face of difficult challenges that may arise.

When you realize you have control over your moods and feelings, your confidence grows and so will your belief in your abilities. There is no more telling yourself that you are a quitter or that you're not ready, not good enough, or not prepared enough to do the work you need to do to accomplish your goals. When you have that negative self-talk under your command, the limits you formerly placed on yourself will be raised substantially.

Your feelings are not your fate.

So remember, your feelings are not your fate. You have access to a higher level of thinking that transcends the way you feel in any given moment. Take advantage of that first thing in the morning to start your day off in the right direction.

Furthermore, make a list of goals for the day. Many personal development authors and students have talked about the importance of having a list of your ultimate goals: an ongoing list of big goals that may likely take years to achieve, but are important to review frequently to give your smaller, daily goals a focus.

Your daily goals should all help to improve you as a person and to get you closer to your bigger goals. Also, they should improve your ability to be persistent as you know that persistence is the game-changer, the differentiator in your journey to success.

> *"If one advances confidently in the direction of his dreams, and endeavors to live the life which he has imagined, he will meet with a success unexpected in common hours."*—Henry David Thoreau

> *"Live the life you imagined."*

You live your life on a day-by-day basis. So if you create a daily program that reflects the work it will take to achieve the life of your dreams, then in a way *you are already living that life.* Because you continue the habits you establish now even when you've reached your goals, you will become the person you are required to be in order to achieve the dream.

Goal setting is the core of creating a daily program. Within that program, you will set achievable goals and gain confidence daily as you reflect on your accomplishments. Besides strengthening your belief in yourself, this also helps you navigate the highs and lows of sustained, creative efforts whether at work, at home, and every other involvement.

You will become the person you are required to be to achieve your dream.

By following a routine, you rely less on your feelings and mood for the day and more on your habits. This is key to concentrating longer, working harder, and getting a much-needed mental breakthrough when the going gets tough.

GOOD SLEEP

Morning routine, healthy diet, exercise, evening routine, good sleep: rinse and repeat the rest of your life.

"Fatigue is the best pillow."—Ben Franklin

Going to bed tired and grateful for the opportunity to rest is best enjoyed after a day of successful work. The more you put into a day, the better you will feel when you lay down at night. Use this truth as a powerful motivator to keep going, especially on a daily basis when you reach certain points in your day when you just want to kick back and take it easy.

This is different from *not resting* when you need to. There are times when you do need to stop and rest, but I'm referring to when you know you could keep working but are tempted by distraction or laziness to stop. Listen to your conscience.

Remember, a good night's sleep and a great morning lies ahead for you if you stay true to your goals and daily program.

EXERCISE

Exercise to increase your dopamine level. We talked about this as part of your tool kit for controlling your mood, but it is also an essential part of your daily program regardless of how you feel in the morning or when you implement your workout.

Somewhere in your daily routine, you must include some form of exercise. It is critical for your physical health, but also your mental alertness and your energy levels and dopamine levels. If you work from a computer like I do, it is even more important to intentionally exercise daily.

Everyone knows various ways to exercise, so I won't go into the specifics. Just find a method of physical training that is doable but challenging, and also somewhat desirable. Taking a 30-minute walk each day reportedly helps you to live a longer life. Think about and then commit to taking a daily walk as a starting point. Start today.

THE POWER OF BEING ORGANIZED

Being organized as you start your day is important as it is a reflection of your mental state. The two feed each other. Your external circumstance can influence your internal and vice versa.

Again, with the goal being to build up your level of persistence, we are often referring to how long you can sit still and concentrate on a task. James Clear, author of *Atomic Habits*, talks about evaluating your work area to see if it is designed to enable you to concentrate. After hearing this, I was prompted to reevaluate my work space and organize a little differently.

Take a couple of minutes to look around where you work. What are some changes you could make? Are there tons of sticky notes laying around with notes you took from phone calls, video calls and other conversations? Are there phone numbers, quotes, and pictures all around you? Are many different electronic devices accessible from where you sit?

Think about what you are trying to accomplish when you sit down to work, and how you can optimize your chances of sticking with it. Sometimes it could be as simple as turning your desk away from the window so you aren't distracted by all you see outside. There may be many different ways you can improve your workspace to aid in your goal to be more persistent and focused.

For instance, if you have multiple task lists laying around, consolidate them. *Consolidate, prioritize, calendarize.* Make sure you write down the due date for when each task needs to be completed. Then when finished with the task, you can cross it off your list and you will have one less distraction.

Regardless of the specifics, it is important to maintain an organized mindset.

Organization helps concentration.

Be careful not to be so organized that you find yourself spending too much time only organizing and not being productive in moving your business forward. Over-preparing for work can be a temptation for those of us who want everything perfect before we begin. Perfectionists often never start for this reason. Remember, you'll never be 100 percent ready. If you are this type of person, break up your day with 15-minute stints of organization work, then come back to the work that moves you closer to your goals.

The fewer distractions around you, the better. When you condition yourself to work for uninterrupted periods of time when you are at a particular place in your house or your business, your body and mind will begin to expect and look forward to concentrating and working while in that place. Condition yourself to concentrate, and the amount of time you will find you have will skyrocket.

Staying focused is a manifestation of persistence.

Being able to stay focused is a manifestation of persistence. Work on making yourself stay in the moment of work and concentration in order to build this characteristic in your life. Learn to really appreciate your ability to focus longer when you are tempted to get up and walk around. When your mind sneaks in a suggestion like, "Why don't you get up and go grab a snack or a drink," react by telling yourself you'll do that in another five minutes. Next time, make it ten minutes. And check the time to make sure you do in fact stay with your task another five minutes.

Many times, you'll stay even longer. The point is to push yourself further and get used to it. You are desensitizing yourself to the call of distraction. This is key. Many people turn to drugs or medication for this ability, but that comes with side effects. Work on doing this naturally and you can get massive benefits as a result.

Desensitize yourself to the call of distraction.

When you are working, rid yourself of any actions that cause you to leave your work, or to daydream about something else, or cause you to work on something else other than what you have begun. It is so easy to become distracted, especially now with our phones on us at all times and the Internet being the fun, distracting, entertaining, and informative rabbit hole that it is.

We use our phones so much, and I am grateful for all the conveniences that technology has brought to us. It is a way of life that we must learn to adapt to in terms of learning how to continue to be productive when all these apps and platforms and communication mediums are fighting for our unending attention.

Build your concentration habits through practice.

For writers, there is a method of writing called writing sprints, where we put phones and any possible distractions aside and write without stopping for a certain amount of time. It may start out as five minutes. The point is to concentrate on the one thing you are doing without outside interference for as long as you can.

All it takes is persistence practice. Practice persistence. Just like anything else, if you practice you will get better over time and with each repetition.

Another benefit of timing your concentration sprints is that you will eventually build up those times long enough to fall into a flow state where you forget about time altogether. When you build yourself up to the point where you can get into that magical place of not caring about anything else except what you are doing for long periods of time, you have reached the place where so much more is possible. And not only that, you will begin to desire being in that state of mind more often; so essentially, you have made the process (the work) your goal.

Now you look forward to the work, not the imagined results.

For example, I was having a hard time sitting down to write this book. This is not uncommon in writers or creators. Steven Pressfield wrote a book about it titled *The War of Art*, which I highly recommend. In his book, he calls the invisible force Resistance, which fights us when we sit down to create. Resistance will do whatever is necessary to keep you from your work for that hour, that day, or even for the week.

The resistance will help you make up all kinds of excuses why you should quit before you start or why you should stop before you have reached your goal for the day. There are methods outlined for fighting this force, but mainly, you have to ignore what you "want" to do in favor of doing what you have to do.

Do what needs to be done and you will feel great having overcome the resistance yet again.

Anyway, I decided to write this book using writing sprints, and that was the breakthrough I needed to get going and get the work done. I set a timer that showed the seconds, for fifteen minutes at a time. Putting a time on my work gave me a sense of urgency, like something bad would happen if I didn't have a certain amount of writing done in that allotted amount of time.

I could see the seconds ticking away.

This little exercise changed my psychology and narrowed my focus into finding a way to share the words I needed to convey this information about persistence.

I was becoming persistent in my effort to write a book on persistence! Go figure.

And that is the kind of thing that happens when you endeavor to work longer at your chosen goal. You come into alignment with the source of energy and those forces propel you forward and give you the insight and concentration needed to continue.

That might sound a little strange or whatever, but try it, it works. Use some kind of trick of the mind to convince yourself that you *must* get a certain chunk of your work done by a certain time, and you will make sure that you do.

The more you keep pushing through, the clearer your path becomes.

There will still be distractions and temptations that can surprise you, but you will get around them because you are focused.

Do the same thing if you are making sales calls, creating content via video or social media, practicing your speaking presentation, or a pitch to a client. Practice without distractions for as long as you can. The longer you can go, the stronger your concentration will become, which is the key to perseverance and success.

You can do this in any career, field of study, industry, or home-based business.

DEVELOP PATIENCE

Persistence is often simply patience. Be patient and stick with any problem long enough to solve it. Patience allows you to sit with a spreadsheet of numbers in front of you long enough to study them and make sense of them and understand the information being presented. Patience allows you to look at a blank document or email and eventually compose the words you need to communicate.

Patience can also be learned through practice. Work on this skill when you are in traffic and in a hurry to get somewhere. Practice when you are waiting in line at the grocery store. Practice when you are listening to another person tell a long and winding story. Practice coming back to the present moment and being patient.

Make yourself physically calm down through deep breathing. Remind yourself that what you are being impatient about is not a big deal. Get your perspective in check.

As you become more patient in the face of trivial problems, you will develop the patience that gives you the staying power to push through obstacles that you will inevitably face as you work toward your goals.

The more patient you can become with your work, the more you will get into a flow state and not think about anything else.

PERSISTENCE IN THE FACE OF TEMPTATION

One evening after a long day at work and in the midst of a 30-day, low carb diet, I rationalized that one night of pizza wouldn't hurt. I pulled into the parking lot of an Italian restaurant and thought about which kind to buy. As I sat there, my conscience nagged at me about not being persistent in completing my diet commitment. Having a pizza was the wrong choice. I wanted to ignore it and just go in anyway, but I buckled my seat belt and drove home.

That I was able to talk myself out of a pizza late in the game on a Friday night, and instead go home and cook a healthy, delicious meal is proof of the power of persistence. Persistence in the face of temptation makes you stronger. Take advantage of those opportunities to grow.

Persistence will be proven and gained as long as you exercise it through both restraint (from vices and distraction) and effort (work and exercise). So in my diet-breaking case, I overcame a massive temptation even in the parking lot that day. I did not break, I did not crack, and as a result, I remained on track.

Have a motivation tool to help you remain focused during times when you don't feel like persevering and working on your goals. It may be a countdown method or a reward method or a quote that you repeat to push yourself into doing what you need to do. Have it ready for times of sluggishness.

Practice it.

The bottom line is we are building—one choice at a time—a character that will endure, one that will not quit. We are forming

Be prepared for when you are your own worst enemy.

the qualities of a person who is relentless, tireless, and not willing to compromise. We are becoming fearless.

It will take time, but time is something we have right now. We're not going to waste it; instead, we will use it to become stronger every single day.

It takes courage not to listen to the voice inside your head offering a way out of the pain, out of the toil, an escape from the monotony, the tedious nature of some of the work that must be done. But once you overcome and silence that voice, you can do it again and again— until you realize that you are actually drawn to what you don't want to do, because now you see challenges where you used to see obstacles. You see opportunities for growth where you used to see problems. All of these small transformations—happening ever so gradually with each choice you make—combine to create a persistence in you that is significant, unusual, and quite to your advantage.

You are creating an unbreakable mindset toward becoming someone who will not be deterred, someone who will do whatever it takes to achieve your goals.

You can become that person. If you don't quit, you *will* become that person. No matter your past, no matter how far behind you think you are now, no matter how far out of character it seems to you to be described as relentless—it is in your future if you start instilling these habits of persistence.

Morning routines, organization, goal-setting, concentration—these are the foundational keys for gaining the power of persistence.

Life is a game of momentum, so get things swinging in your direction by starting a positive morning routine tomorrow. Set your alarm clock now.

TIME IS TICKING

You know what to do. This is a starting point, this is your reminder, the sign you've been looking for—this is when you stop quitting on yourself and go hard after what you are being called to do.

Time is ticking and you no longer have a choice. You have been given the answers and you have been called to act. You can no longer ignore the small yet mighty voice in your head calling you to greater things in life. If you do, your conscience will never allow you to have peace, no matter what you do to quell its nagging call.

When you begin the daily work of instilling the positive habits noted in this chapter, the next step is to get help from your subconscious mind. Few people take advantage of the power of the subconscious mind, which gives you an incredible edge when you practice some of the techniques described in the following pages.

The effects of using your mind to influence your body and the direction of your days is nothing short of miraculous. An experience or two will confirm once and for all the higher operating power that exists in the universe. When you act in alignment with your calling, you are in sync with who you are supposed to be. And the possibilities that arise from living in line with your calling are endless.

Stay tuned in, and let's get into the mental work that goes into gaining the power of persistence.

REFLECTION AND GOAL SETTING

Questions for reflection and goal setting:

1. What are your current daily habits, beginning in the morning?

2. What would you ideally do as part of your morning routine?

3. What are some habits you would like to instill that would help increase your current level of persistence?

4. What causes you to stop working most frequently?

5. What distractions do you have that often grab your attention when you are bored, or feeling down?

6. What goals can you set for longer periods of concentration? Give the context and specific lengths of time.

CHAPTER TWO

ACTIVATE THE POWER OF YOUR MIND

"It is the power of the mind to be unconquerable."

—SENECA

CLARIFY YOUR VISION

Many times, we quit because our vision is not clear. What is your vision, and what steps will you take to make your vision a reality?

Remember the larger goal. You have to be super clear on what you want so that it can be the guiding light when you want to put off the smaller, seemingly insignificant daily tasks.

When you can come back to your grand vision that you have for your life, it reminds you of why it is important to do the things you don't want to do.

Don't let yourself be talked into quitting on a goal. Don't negotiate with yourself to get out of finishing what you started. When you let yourself quit once, you make it easier to quit again.

When you don't follow through on doing what you said you would do, you are subconsciously telling yourself that you cannot be trusted, and that your word is not important. This comes through in your interactions with others as well. It is important that you hit your daily goals no matter what. You said it to yourself, you gave your word. If you cannot keep your word to yourself, you won't keep it with others.

If you don't have confidence in yourself, no one else will either.

Anyway, clarify your vision. Write it down, say it out loud. Believe you will accomplish it one day. Make the details memorable and visible if you can. Let your vision be the last thing you think about before you go to sleep and the first thing you think about in the morning.

USING THE SUBCONSCIOUS MIND

Speaking of when you go to sleep, this is part of the power of your subconscious mind: repeat to yourself something you want to happen tomorrow over and over again just before you go to sleep. Start this when you are close to dozing off, the lights are off in your room, and you are rolling over or ready to fall asleep, start repeating something you want to accomplish, or something you want to believe/improve about yourself over and over again as you drift out of consciousness.

This repetition imprints those ideas on your subconscious mind and transfers these thoughts and beliefs to your conscious mind—and the next day you begin to realize that what you spoke has come to fruition.

As you are doing this at night, it doesn't have to be audible, it can be a phrase that you say over and over again in your mind. The point is to keep it short and repeatable and keep it cycling in your mind as you drift off. I have heard of someone simply repeating that they would sell more products the next day, and sure enough, it happened.

So try it out. Many people dismiss these kinds of tactics as unrealistic. But because they don't try them, they never really know. Don't be the person who rejects what you don't know out of hand. Give it a try; you have nothing to lose. Tell your subconscious that you are a relentless, persistent person. Tell yourself you will not quit as you go to sleep tonight. Come up with some related mantra, repeat it to yourself as you fall asleep, and watch how your day goes tomorrow.

FAITH

"Faith is a state of mind which may be induced, or created, by affirmation or repeated instructions to the subconscious mind…"—Napoleon Hill, *Think and Grow Rich*

To truly gain persistence, begin by establishing habits that strengthen your body and mind. The result is that you gain faith in yourself by sticking to your habits, building up daily "wins," and teaching your subconscious mind to change your internal dialogue.

The way to influence your subconscious begins with the actions I have described. Napoleon Hill continues, *"Repetition of affirmation of orders to your subconscious mind is the only known method of voluntary development of the emotion of faith."*

It's not hypnosis; it's repetition and the subtle art of inspiring and controlling your own beliefs.

Faith, like persistence, is a state of mind. As such, it is a state you can induce by your own actions.

Look at how people change by being desensitized. For example, in the Navy Seals training programs, the trainees are exposed to extremely stressful situations that assault all of their senses at once and make it hard to think. Through repeated exposure to frightful, emotionally stressful situations, the men and women are eventually able to remain calm and think clearly.

This is exactly what you are doing for yourself. You are repeatedly exposing your subconscious mind to an idea that will eventually take to be a truth and will transfer that belief to your conscious mind as faith, into physical reality through your subsequent actions.

This works with negative thoughts as well, which is why many people lack confidence and feel that they are not good enough. Many individuals repeat negative statements to themselves. These statements are adopted as truth by the subconscious mind and translated into actions taken by orders from the conscious mind of people who then believe these negative thoughts about themselves.

For example, one person might have had a negative experience speaking in front of the class in high school. It may have caused embarrassment, a poor grade from the teacher, and perhaps further comments from peers. As a result, the student thought, "I'm not good at speaking in front of people," or, "I'm no good at giving presentations," and all kinds of other incorrect assumptions or descriptions that may not really be true.

Nevertheless, we can make almost anything true of ourselves in our mind.

Activating the power of your mind is an incredible opportunity—a way to rewrite your story. Take advantage of it starting today!

Imagine you are already living the life of your dreams. Imagine you are already the kind of person who could achieve those great things you have envisioned. Do the things that person would do. Tell yourself who you are by your actions and by your own repeated thoughts. Do not let your past or others define you.

> *"Remember, your subconscious mind does not engage in proving whether your thoughts are good or bad, true or false, but it responds according to the nature of your thoughts or suggestions."*—Joseph Murphy, PhD, *The Power of Your Subconscious Mind*

On the negative side, this truth is seen in what is known as the scarcity mindset. Some people do not attract wealth and prosperity to themselves because they are always focused on saving money motivated by a fear of poverty. They are constantly telling themselves they need money saved in case something bad happens; and as a result, their subconscious mind reinforces the idea that they do not have enough money.

That doesn't mean people should be reckless and not save money, but it points to a mindset that reinforces what we feed it. People who are extremely frugal could often be making much more money if they weren't so focused on the fear of not having it.

Anyway, the point is that our subconscious is recording our thoughts and indirectly creating your reality. So it is critical that we control our thoughts and our words.

EVERY WORD COUNTS

Think about all the words we waste. When you are talking negatively to yourself, you are wasting your words. You are wasting potential positive influence and change.

Burn it in your mind to REVERSE your negative thoughts. *Every time.* Make it a goal just for one hour today to acknowledge every negative thought and then state the reverse of the statement to yourself whenever it happens.

For example, when you think about a phone call you are dreading, change the thought to, "I'm looking forward to this phone call because of the growth opportunities that will come from an uncomfortable situation." Customize your reversal of language to your own needs, but make sure with each and every negative thought, you completely say the opposite of it in your mind, the second it pops into your head. Especially if it is about yourself.

CHECK YOUR SELF-TALK DAILY

If you have a video call with clients whom you have not talked to before and they are particularly successful and demanding, and it feels like they are operating on a level of business that you have not arrived at yet, you will likely dredge up some insecurity thoughts about how you are not ready yet, you're not as successful, and you will probably make a fool of yourself.

With all negative personal thoughts about your own abilities, flip them to the opposite. Repeat to yourself, "I *am* ready," and, "I *am* confident in my ability to handle this call and talk to these clients in a way that makes them happy to be doing business with me."

Simply make yourself believe something different from what you have been telling yourself up to this point.

It can feel overwhelming because we are often talking about years of mental conditioning where we have not only repeated and believed negative things about ourselves, but our actions as a result may have established quite a few bad habits like overeating, overthinking, abusing drugs, etc. Be patient with yourself.

All of these actions will be addressed by establishing your morning routine and the persistence-inducing habits discussed in Chapter 1. And the mental part of what drives those habits is what you are addressing right now. It begins with programming your subconscious mind that is in process 24-7 to imprint different thoughts on your conscious mind, which is the one you are using right now as you think about what to have for dinner or whether or not you should continue reading this or any other daily activity that requires thought.

This mental reprogramming is a daily effort.

Reversing negative thoughts into positive thoughts is an action of your conscious mind that is critical to your success. It helps to improve your mood, your energy levels, and the chance that you will persist in any given effort to achieve your goals.

"We injure ourselves by the negative ideas which we entertain. How often have you wounded yourself by

getting angry, fearful, jealous, or vengeful? These are the poisons that enter your subconscious mind. You were not born with these negative attitudes. Feed your subconscious mind life-giving thoughts, and you will wipe out all the negative patterns lodged therein. As you continue to do this, all the past will be wiped out and remembered no more."—Joseph Murphy, *The Power of Your Subconscious Mind*

WHEN TALKING WITH OTHERS

Reversing negative thought patterns is also critical when talking to others. There can be a pleasant feeling of catharsis or validation when you complain to someone you trust. You can talk negatively about your work situation, a project, a colleague, or some upsetting event that happened to you.

Who were you before you told yourself untrue stories about your failures and your past?

It's okay to talk about things, to get things off your chest—but try to limit the amount of complaining you do. Make sure your conversations about problems are solutions-centered. You may have a friend or partner whom you trust with conversations full of complaining or negativity, just be aware that the complaint-filled conversations are not becoming habitual. It is easy to find a source of pleasure in venting, but it is not usually a productive activity.

If you want to become someone who achieves more through persistence, rid yourself of negativity as much as possible. At the very next opportunity, practice spinning your conversation positively when you are tempted to complain about something or someone.

Remember, the people who achieve success are not focused on other people and what they are doing wrong, high-achievers are busy working on their own positive goals.

REVISIT YOUR VISION
OF THE LIFE YOU IMAGINE

As we wrap up this chapter, remember the principle of autosuggestion as it impacts your subconscious mind. This is a valuable, constant tool to use throughout your journey of becoming persistent.

Second, take a few minutes to revisit your vision of what you want to achieve in your life. Write down the specifics, but this time write them in the present tense. For example, "I am a successful business owner and my business is doing $100,000 a year in sales. I live in Hawaii and work from home. I am a confident person and can talk to anyone. I'm feeling good about being in the best physical shape I have ever been, etc." This kind of affirmation makes your vision real for you and also impacts your subconscious.

Writing your vision, talking about it, working on your daily habits, your subconscious mind—it all starts to feel repetitive. That's because it is. That is the secret to why it works. You are rewiring the way your brain works so that you can essentially become a different person who thinks in a way that will influence action that brings you the success you want.

When you start combining the effects of your new habits, your new thought processes, and your subsequent faith in yourself, you have unleashed a new kind of power that you have not yet experienced. But you will experience it if you continue down this path.

Be persistent in your efforts to establish your habits and to reprogram your subconscious mind. It might feel boring at times, mundane and useless, but catch yourself when you start to think that way and reverse it. Your boredom and your pain and discomfort will lead you to greater achievements and success in life.

And there is only one rule—*Do not quit.*

There may be setbacks that come your way from external, uncontrollable sources, so you need to be prepared to be strong enough to keep going in the face of obstacles. You are getting stronger and stronger through your habits and self-talk, and soon you will be unfazed and unstoppable no matter what life throws at you.

You will not self-sabotage. You will not stop just because of your feelings. Your purpose is higher than your impulses, stronger than your desire for comfort.

When it rains, we work. When the sun shines, we work. When it's cold outside, we work. When trouble arises, we work. When our mind is in tatters, we work. When the body feels broken, we work. When we are depressed, we work. When we can't think straight due to stress, we work. Especially when we want to quit, we work.

Your purpose is higher than your impulses, stronger than your desire for comfort.

And so you repeat mantras like this, say these lines over and over again to yourself until it sticks in your subconscious mind and you begin to actually believe what you are saying. Once you start believing it, you'll know it because you will start to take action that reflects this belief about yourself and who you are and what you do or don't do.

It starts with planting the thoughts in your mind through these techniques of autosuggestion. Your body will take care of the rest naturally. So work on autosuggestions as often as you can. You can use this strategy for all kinds of goals within your personal development.

GAINING THE POWER OF PERSISTENCE

In this case, we are working on gaining the power of persistence and it is important to get your mind right. Also, persistence is of such high value, that it will take a high level of sincerity and desire to achieve it. So, begin with the two pillars of mental strength: 1) autosuggestion; and 2) a crystal clear vision of your goal.

Remember, you are no longer the kind of person who quits, so begin by getting that straight in your mind. Write and repeat some lines like the following:

I do not quit, do not give up in the face of failure.

If I have made mistakes, I will try again and appreciate the opportunity to do better next time.

I will not give up when in doubt. I will push through to the next day to build up my strength so I'm not even tempted next time.

I am gaining belief in myself that is so strong that I am becoming too tough for external circumstances to affect me like they used to—and that feels great! I will do more to experience the satisfaction of a job well done.

The more I repeat the actions that lead to that feeling, the more I create a habit that is good for my growth.

Persistence then is a habit we can establish within ourselves that becomes our defining characteristic. Imagine if you were someone who simply did not quit on yourself or your dreams. What could you accomplish? How much of your work for tomorrow would already be done today?

What if you were someone who continues to work on your goals while other people party because it's the weekend. Or people take a nap because they are tired. Or they sleep in because they don't have to get up for their day job. Do you only get up early to make money at your day job? Essentially you are willing to get up early for someone else, why not for yourself?

Imagine the massive possibilities of gaining hours in your week and days in your month just by getting up a little earlier to put effort into accomplishing your dreams. Persistence will do this for you.

You are a persistent person, which is why you win. You are not going to quit anything today. And your success will be worth all the effort. Believe it.

BREAK DOWN YOUR WORK

A lot of your ability to be persistent and achieve your goals comes down to your outlook. Knowing it is a mental game, you have to make it a priority to use psychology to your advantage. For example, many prisoners confined to their cells do high-volume bodyweight exercises (like push-ups) to gain physical strength.

Taking push-ups for instance, if you look at doing 500 push-ups, it might seem overwhelming. But if you break it down into sets, it becomes more manageable. If you do what is called 30 down push-ups, you do 30, then you do 29, then you do 28 and on down to 1. And the result of doing those sets will be 465 push-ups. Again, it seems like a ton all at once, but break your work down in various creative ways, and you might be surprised how you can do much more than what you thought.

Use your mind to help you attain your goals by finding ways to make it manageable mentally first.

OVERALL POSITIVE OUTLOOK

Jesse Cole, the owner and founder of the Savannah Bananas, a minor league baseball team in Georgia, has made it his goal to reinvigorate the culture surrounding his team and increase attendance at the games. He uses all kinds of entertainment antics akin to those of the Harlem Globetrotters in basketball.

Running out of money with a failing team and deserted stadium in 2015, Cole used various tactics to energize and speed up the game—a style he calls Banana Ball—and introduce interaction with the fans to create an exciting atmosphere that has resulted in constantly sold-out games and a huge online following since 2017.

When asked about stunts or antics that went wrong, he answers: *"My mind doesn't work like that. I'm just so focused on the next at-bat that I don't process or think about failure too much, because then it will keep you from trying new things."* (Success magazine May/June 2023)

Many times, we are not succeeding because we are constantly imagining and thinking of all the things that could go or did go wrong. We focus on all the reasons something won't work. This is similar to the scarcity mindset. If you think this way, of course you will not achieve your goals. Your mind is running all the negative scenarios in your thoughts, and your actions—or lack thereof—reflect that story.

The antidote is to only imagine that it *will* work, that you *will* be successful, and *will* achieve your goals. Keep that in your mind always, regardless of what people say to you. Don't procrastinate due to self-doubt. Do the work *you know you need to do* so that you move forward. When you imagine and envision reaching your goals, don't even think about your plan not working.

This is your calling.

You *will* win.

REFLECTION AND GOAL SETTING

Questions for reflection and goal setting:

1. Can you picture your goals clearly?

2. How is your self-talk? Mostly positive or mostly negative?

3. What is a go-to quote you can use when you want to quit next time?

4. In what ways can you use your mind to help you in your daily goals?

5. Are you working on programming your subconscious mind?

6. Do you picture your ideas working out, or do you tend to find all the flaws in them?

7. Think of some ways to break down a daunting task you have on your list.

CHAPTER THREE

USE PAIN AND FAILURE AS MOTIVATION

"One mistake does not have to rule a person's entire life."
—JOYCE MEYER

*"I have failed over and over again in my life.
And that is why I succeed."*
—MICHAEL JORDAN

Failure and setbacks can be extremely helpful in turning you into a persistent person who achieves goals.

Failure is an inevitable part of life—but how we respond to failure determines our future success. Perseverance is the ability to keep going, despite setbacks and failures. It's the determination to overcome obstacles and achieve success. If we want to become persistent and achieve our goals, we must come up with a plan to use our failures in life to motivate us forward.

How do you do that? *Change your perspective!*

It's essential to change your mindset from failure to success. Instead of seeing failure as a negative experience, view it as an opportunity for growth and learning. Be alright with making mistakes.

In fact, work on getting your mind to the point where you *want* to make mistakes. When you aren't making any mistakes at all, you aren't making progress either. Sometimes we need to get out there and try some things and make some mistakes in order to learn.

Speaking of learning, it's crucial to learn from failure. Reflect on the experience, analyze what went wrong, and how you can make improvements for next time. Here's a simple three-step process to implement after each so-called failure:

1. Analyze what went wrong.
2. Reflect on ideas and thoughts around the mistake and take notes.
3. Come up with a plan to improve.

When you start using this process every time you make a mistake in your business or personal growth process, failure can be seen as an opportunity for self-reflection, growth, and development. You will begin to look forward to using all failure as a learning opportunity, and apply the lessons learned to future endeavors.

"Failure is only the opportunity to begin again, this time more intelligently."—Henry Ford

Then, set realistic goals. Setting realistic goals can prevent failure from becoming overwhelming and demotivating. It's essential to set goals that are challenging but achievable. Small successes can lead to greater ones, and each failure can be viewed as a stepping stone toward success.

"Success is the ability to go from one failure to another with no loss of enthusiasm."—Winston Churchill

Develop a support system. Surround yourself with people who will encourage and motivate you. Share your failures with them and ask for their help and advice. A supportive community can provide the necessary encouragement and motivation to keep going. Even if it is just one other person, consult with someone about your goals.

> *Surround yourself with people who are driven and supportive.*

Napoleon Hill called this concept the "Master Mind" in his famous bestseller, *Think and Grow Rich* where he writes: "The Master Mind may be defined as: Coordination of knowledge and effort, in a spirit of harmony, between two or more people for the attainment of a definite purpose."

Hill goes on to write:

> "No two minds ever come together without thereby creating a third invisible, intangible force which may be likened to a third mind…. Men and women take on the nature and the habits and the power of thought of those with whom they associate in a spirit of sympathy and harmony."

So surround yourself with people who are driven and who are supportive. This will not only be a source of ideas and inspiration for you, it will also be encouragement for you during the tough times.

Then, stay focused on your vision. Remember why you started and keep your eyes on the prize. It's easy to get demotivated when facing failure, but it's essential to keep the end goal in mind. Focus on the bigger picture and keep moving forward, even when facing obstacles or dealing with temporary failure.

When you overcome challenges, you get the momentum swinging your way again.

You are cultivating resilience. Resilience becomes the ability to bounce back from setbacks and failures. It's just another form of persistence like patience. Resilience is the capacity to adapt to change and overcome adversity.

When you overcome challenges, you get the momentum swinging your way again.

For me as a writer, I have to stop walking away from the keyboard when I'm frustrated and the words aren't coming. We really have to work at it and push through the annoyances in order to get going in a rhythm and get into the flow state. Failure is often just a pause, a time to remember what you already know and keep going.

> *"Perseverance is failing 19 times and succeeding the 20th."*—Julie Andrews

Wes Watson, now a successful fitness coach, spent ten years in prison. During his incarceration and after a few years of fighting and using drugs (even in prison), he decided to turn his life around and become healthy and disciplined.

He used his anger problem—what partially led him to commit the violent act that led him to prison—to fuel his workouts and his desire to turn into a rare individual. After another five or six years, he was released, was *Remember that failure is not the end, but part of the journey toward greatness.* sober, extremely fit, and ready to help others. He had spent his time reading uplifting material, working out, and reflecting on his regrets and his internal state, getting rid of negativity through his exercise.

Now he is a millionaire fitness coach who helps thousands of people drop their bad habits and find freedom and fulfillment through a disciplined lifestyle.

Find the motivation within yourself by looking at the things in your life or about you that you want to change.

Consider your failures and find within them something you can use to motivate yourself to do better. Evaluate where you went wrong and design another attempt that is stronger based on what you now know. Failures, then, are opportunities to gain an advantage the next time you try.

Don't waste any time wallowing in disappointment. Learn what you can and begin planning your next venture right away.

Use character flaws to your advantage. If you have anxiety, pour those anxious thoughts into a form of exercise and talk positively to yourself while you are training. Stop telling yourself you have anxiety and begin telling yourself you are excited. The physiological processes of nervousness and excitement are the same.

Find a way to spin your negative thoughts to a positive idea in your mind.

Remember that persistence is a skill that can be developed and you are becoming a persistent person one hour, one day at a time. The sacrifice is minimal and the rewards are many.

If you are prone to addiction, turn your addictive behavior to exercise and work rather than substances. Your obsession with whatever your poison is can be powerful when channeled into a productive action—and actually gives you an edge over the average person.

There are so many ways in which the attributes you used to always tell yourself were less than desirable can be used for good. And remember, other people struggle with the same things you do; so if you can heal yourself through persistent constructive behavior and goal achievement, you can share what worked for you and help others in the process.

ATTITUDE TOWARD SETBACKS

Jocko Willink, a Navy SEAL and bestselling author of *Extreme Ownership* and other titles, talks about how he solves problems with one word. When someone comes to him with a problem or an issue that will cause delays or otherwise negative impacts on a project or an initiative, he responds first with a one-word answer.

The one word? "Good"

So every time he runs into a problem, his immediate mental response is to see it as *good* so that he then can use the opportunity to improve his approach, system, or whatever it is that needs to be addressed in order to avoid the problem in the future.

When you condition your mind to see negatives as positives, the world of opportunity and growth opens up. Persistence starts with your mindset. This reprogramming of your mind will help you overcome so many trivial and big issues that arise and threaten to derail you from your goals.

If you typically get stressed out over certain things, change your mindset to say "good," when stressors confront you, and your mindset will be changed and you will be able to see a way to help solve the problem. In the process of working through problems, you become stronger, more resilient which are essential characteristics of becoming persistent in your daily life.

So start with your attitude when you are faced with setbacks. Don't worry about anything else, just say, "Good."

> *"When we are strong, we are always much greater than the things that happen to us."*
> —Thomas Merton

NO FAILURE EXCEPT QUITTING

You cannot fail. The only failure is if you quit. It's harder to live life knowing that you quit. Keep pushing forward.

Quitting means regretting. So, if you cannot find another reason to keep going today, do it to avoid regret. This is one of those mantras to repeat to yourself whenever you can, "there is no failure except quitting."

If you remember this throughout the good and bad times, you will have inspiration to keep going. You are burning the bridge behind you. You are committing.

Put this line on a sign and post it somewhere prominent in your work area. You are not someone who quits, that is the simple truth.

Burn the bridge behind you—commit to the future.

STOP SEEKING COMFORT
AND A PROBLEM-FREE LIFE

Another mindset adjustment to get out of the way is that when you have goals to achieve, you have to be purpose driven. You cannot be out seeking pleasure or wanting to live a constantly comfortable life.

Adopt the mentality of being tough. Start telling yourself that you can handle adverse situations, uncomfortable situations so that you are mentally ready to actually handle them when you are faced with them.

The goal with this part of your persistence journey is to develop a thick skin mentality.

> *"You can get a lot of power through misery."*
> —David Goggins

It's about reshaping your thoughts when it comes to pain and failure and misery. Discomfort is your motivation. When everyone else would quit, you use that fatigue and that despair to move you forward.

> *"The enemy has to know you are not going to give up."*—David Goggins

Once you convince yourself that you are relentless, you will fear nothing. You will fear no one, and you will have broken through what used to stop you and turn you around. Develop an unbreakable mind by pushing yourself through the limits, the points where you used to quit. Practice on little things like exercise, cleaning, and tedious work.

If you can start being a person who doesn't stop when others do, you will build a following. You will notice more and more people wanting to know what makes you special. People will be inspired and they will follow your lead. Change yourself into someone more powerful and more persistent, and the world will make way for you.

Yes, there will be unforeseen challenges and changes, but now you are mentally tough and you are prepared to move through them to achieve your goals.

When you change yourself into someone more powerful and more persistent, the world will make way for you.

PERSISTENCE REINFORCES YOUR PURPOSE

Your purpose in life is to be the best you can be. Follow this purpose throughout your life, and you will always find the courage and strength to keep going. Someone is counting on you. Someone is going to emulate your action and attitude in each stage and circumstance of life.

I asked my daughter what persistence means. She said it means to keep going after failing multiple times or when obstacles come your way. She's right. A simple definition for me to remember.

Be persistent for your loved ones. Set the example and live it out.

How to reinforce your purpose and increase your persistence:

1. Write it down.
2. Practice not quitting on small, mundane tasks.
3. Think of the people who may follow your example.

WHEN QUITTING IS A GOOD THING

Now that I've gone on and on about not quitting ever, let's talk about a couple of times when you should quit.

1. *It's good to quit bad habits.* Anything that weakens you, your willpower, or causes you regret after having done

it—drop those activities right now. Start today. And if you pick it up in a week or so, drop it again.

Do not give up trying to quit your bad habits and eventually your persistence will pay off and the habit will be gone for good. Again, it's an attitude—persistence. You are trying to get to the point where you feel pleasure in your efforts to overcome what is easy but bad for you. When you can overcome temptations on a daily basis and take pride in those moments, you'll have turned a corner in gaining this skill of persistence.

You must know whether what you are planning to persist in is the right thing to do. Evaluate your motives. Is it what you are being called to do, or are you just trying to do it to make money? Is your goal ego-driven? Are you sacrificing an important relationship over your goal? Make sure you acknowledge signs that are telling you to change direction.

I know this sounds ambiguous and it is, but lean on people you trust. Consult with your partner and or support group on issues where there seems to be a fork in the road. Ultimately, listen to that small voice in your head that you know is your conscience reminding you of your values, your purpose, and the things in life you should not negotiate on.

2. *It's good to quit if you are headed down the wrong path.* If you should quit and take another path, listen to your conscience and take the other route.

But if you just want to quit because you are disappointed with the results or it's taking too long or because you don't feel like doing what you need to do, keep going.

TRY HARDER

We are living in a world where it is becoming popular to quit your job or to not try as hard as you can. It's easier to get by not doing as much, for now. There are more people "phoning in their work," doing things halfway.

Right now, all you have to do to stand out as exceptional is to work a little harder than the average person.

But don't stop there. Demand more of yourself. To try harder means to show gratitude for being alive. It means you believe in yourself and your dreams. It means you are worth the effort you are putting forth. Don't get caught comparing yourself to someone else who has much lower standards than you. Be honest with yourself. Are you working up to your potential? Are you satisfied with the amount of effort you are putting forward?

Showing others that you are willing to work when others are slacking gives inspiration and hope to people you don't even know. Doing the work you are called to do and following your purpose with all your heart to be the best person you can be is a selfless act. Why selfless? Because it means you are willing to do what you don't feel like doing in order to become the person who can help others. You are sacrificing what you would rather do to do what you need to do to be a light and motivator to those around you.

USE THE EMOTION OF AGGRESSION

Jocko Willink also teaches that aggression is an innate part of us, and some of us have more aggressive tendencies than others obviously. But aggression can be trained for a positive outcome. Aggression can be a good thing if we use it to control situations that we used to leave to happenstance. For example, in military operations almost nothing will go as planned unless there is force behind what needs to happen in a certain way. By the same token, your life can be controlled with training in the mental department.

Jocko explains, "You can start to think with an aggressive mindset which is, 'I am going to take action. I am going to overcome obstacles. I am going to push through roadblocks. I'm not going to take no for an answer.'"

You cannot quit just because you hear "no." And just because you run into an obstacle, you can't allow your mind to think about quitting. Train yourself to be more aggressive in your thinking and you won't be so easily discouraged or derailed.

STAY WITH IT A LITTLE LONGER

The more you persist and the more you do things despite your desire to quit or do something else, the more ideas will come and the more breakthroughs and deep insights you will have.

Overcome your body's desires through the power of your will. Every time you use your willpower, you are eventually rewarded with ideas and events that you wouldn't have had otherwise. So don't quit just because you feel like quitting.

Concentration brings forth creativity. Thoughts are generated through persistent effort that otherwise would not have happened.

The mind is always at work. You are always busy thinking about something, so you have to control your mind and concentrate your attention to get something done. If you have too many competing desires about which you are trying to be persistent, you won't get anything done. You have to decide which ones are to be pursued and which should be dropped or put on hold for now.

Joseph Murphy, in his famous book *The Power of Your Subconscious Mind*, puts it this way:

> *"If you get into a taxi and give a half dozen different directions to the driver in five minutes, he would become hopelessly confused and probably would refuse to take you anywhere. It is the same when working with your subconscious mind. There must be a clear-cut idea in your mind."*

This is why it is critical to build a persistence mindset through working harder longer and developing the power of will. It is preparation for success in reaching your goals. This is why exercising daily is important, getting up early is important. These are activities we don't necessarily want to do, but the more we do them, the tougher and more prepared we are.

Successful people have not lived every day seeking comfort and the easy route. Instead, they intentionally do hard things daily and develop a stronger will and more persistent character. This is key for you as well.

"There may be no heroic connotation to the word **persistence,** *but the quality is to the character of man what carbon is to steel."*—Napoleon Hill, *Think and Grow Rich*

So essentially, what you are doing so far on your path to becoming persistent is visualizing what you want, who you want to become, then working through autosuggestion and influencing the subconscious mind to develop the faith that you ARE that person, and then using failure and obstacles as something that drives you forward.

When you are in the autosuggestion/mental preparation mode, it doesn't matter if what you are saying about yourself is true. It only matters that it gets you to keep going when you would have quit. Do this repeatedly and you will find those things you said before are in fact true of you.

Repetition builds strength.

You've got this!

REFLECTION AND GOAL SETTING

Questions for reflection and goal setting:

1. What failures have you experienced and what did you learn from them?

2. What are your flaws? How can you use them to your advantage?

3. Are you afraid to fail? What is your perspective and your reaction when things do not go as planned?

4. How can you improve your outlook regarding adverse situations and events?

5. How do you view living comfortably? When you find yourself seeking pleasure more than following your purpose?

6. What are some tough goals you can set that will be hard to accomplish but will improve your character if you persevere and attain them?

CHAPTER FOUR

STRENGTHEN YOUR BELIEF IN YOURSELF

"Once we believe in ourselves, we can risk curiosity, wonder, spontaneous delight, or any experience that reveals the human spirit."

—E. E. CUMMINGS

"Perseverance is another word for faith."

—EARL NIGHTINGALE

Believing in yourself is critical for developing persistence and achieving your goals. The confidence in your abilities, talents, and potential gives you the power to keep going when you want to quit.

To increase your belief in yourself, focus on your strengths. Identify your strengths and focus on them. What are you good at doing? What skill gives you satisfaction when you use it to help other people? Recognize the unique skills and talents that you possess and develop them further. Celebrate your accomplishments, no matter how small, and use them as a source of motivation to achieve greater things.

Challenge negative self-talk. Negative self-talk can erode your self-confidence and belief in yourself. It's important to challenge negative thoughts and replace them with positive ones, as discussed previously.

> *"If you hear a voice within you say 'you cannot paint,' then by all means paint, and that voice will be silenced."*—Vincent Van Gogh

Prove to yourself your competence by doing the thing you are doubtful about. Replace self-doubt with self-affirmations and surround yourself with positive people who will encourage and motivate you. Keep in mind your vision of who you want to become.

Remember to set achievable goals. Setting and hitting achievable goals can boost your belief in yourself. Choose goals that challenge you but are within reach. Break down larger goals into smaller, manageable ones, and celebrate each success along the way. Each accomplishment will strengthen your belief in yourself and motivate you to achieve more.

Take some risks to increase your confidence and belief in yourself. Step out of your comfort zone and try new things.

Failure is a natural part of the process as we established in the previous chapter. Nothing is guaranteed anyway. We often imagine security in living risk-averse lives, but anything can happen still. Take calculated risks and use each experience to build your confidence and belief in yourself.

> *"You sometimes lose by taking risks, but you always lose by holding back."*—Rachel Wolchin

Take care of your physical, emotional, and mental well-being. Prioritize rest, exercise, and healthy eating. Practice mindfulness and meditation to reduce stress and improve mental clarity. When you feel good about yourself, your confidence and belief in yourself will also grow.

All of these steps will help you strengthen your belief in yourself, and that is the crucial element of persistence. You believe you can. That's what it all boils down to and what will put you on a different level from where you are now.

You can believe you can.

When you are consistent with your habits, positive with your self-talk, and strong in the face of failure, the next step is developing your belief in your ability. All those prior efforts led to this place. And now it is not just faith, you actually do believe in your abilities, because you have done the work to earn that belief. You have done the work to improve what you do, to be the best at what you do.

KEEP YOUR WORD

It is essential that you persist when you say to yourself and or others that you are going to do something. Saying something and then following through is how you build trust and confidence in yourself. On the other hand, if you often say things like, "I'm going to start exercising next month," or, "I'm going to go 30 days sober," or, "I'm going to make 25 social media posts this week," and then you don't follow through, you weaken your belief in yourself and show others that you don't keep your word.

When this happens often enough, your mind will imprint that you are okay with not keeping your promise or following through, which will inevitably lead to thinking that it is okay to quit the process of achieving the goals you set. The next time you set a goal and then run into obstacles or feelings of wanting to quit, it will be easier to find the excuse to do so.

In the big picture, you are programming your mind to believe that this is alright and that quitting is an aspect of your personality. Again, sometimes it is the right choice to quit if you realize you are going down the wrong career path or if another opportunity presents itself, but in the daily habits that will only help you grow, it is important to keep your word to yourself, and to others.

OVERCOMING

What do you know you have to overcome in order to reach your goals?

Make a list of the obstacles in as much detail as possible. Is it the habit of self-doubt? Is it a vice such as alcohol or video games or binge watching your favorite shows? Think about what you turn to for stress relief.

You need to overcome whatever is holding you back from doing the work that takes you closer to your ultimate goal. Find books about it. There are video courses that can help. Do something daily that helps to free yourself from your self-imposed restraints.

Strengthening your belief in yourself is about learning to overcome difficulties so you can trust that you have the ability to do so.

A lot of doubt comes in because we have not tested ourselves to make sure that we have the ability to follow through with what needs to be done in any given situation. All it takes to get this ability is to self-inflict adversity into your life and then overcome it using your mind and willpower. We'll talk more about willpower in upcoming pages, but the mental part is just as important.

Through practice we gain belief. Through autosuggestion we reinforce that belief. So if you want to be someone who doesn't fall apart when under pressure, put yourself into high-pressure situations to test yourself. It may mean joining the military. It may be taking a high-pressure sales job. It may mean doing an extremely hard workout program.

As you progress through the physical aspects of over-coming difficulty, your belief in self will increase. This is confidence-building through action.

Keep your goal of persistence in line with your vision. Throughout the days, weeks, and months that you are working on persistence, remember your vision. Keep your vision strong and clear so that you remember why you are pushing through one more call, one more repetition, one more email, and focus on making sure the work you are doing remains in line with your ultimate goal for your life.

It's easy to get caught up in the practice of one activity or another and forget why you are doing it. When that happens, distraction can easily creep in and you can lose days and weeks of the work you should be putting in toward your goal.

WHEN YOU FEEL ANGRY

When you feel frustrated with someone, with yourself, or with a situation, do not throw in the towel. Keep pushing yourself through with physical exercise, if possible, and your work secondarily. You have to find a place to put your negative energy to productive use.

Don't dwell on the worrisome or negative thoughts that keep coming to mind, especially if they are about something that happened earlier in the day that upset you. You have already moved on from that experience. That moment is gone forever and all that you have right now is the moment you are in.

Are you going to waste your present moment bringing yourself down by choosing to stay in a negative memory? The thoughts will keep coming back to haunt you for as long as you keep giving them the time.

Stop the cycle of rehashing what happened by throwing yourself into work or exercise or helping others. Find some activity to take you away from the aggravating thoughts you are experiencing—but don't give up on the day or your goals.

Keep going!

Later today, you'll feel better and tomorrow will be a brand-new day. Let the frustration pass and live your life from the present. Once you are able to push through situations like this, when the next one comes, you will be more confident in yourself to get through it without quitting on your goals for the day.

Turning anger into inspiration or reframing it entirely into something positive is another vital tool to keep ready. When you face challenging situations, flip them around. It is incredibly empowering and goes a long way toward helping you to believe in yourself even more.

AVOID JEALOUSY

"Envy comes from people's ignorance of, or lack of belief in, their own gifts."—Jean Vanier

Many times when we criticize others or find ourselves feeling resentful of another person's success, it's because we don't believe in our own abilities. We are not focused on doing our work, so we look at and evaluate other people's work instead.

Anytime you catch yourself talking about someone else in a negative light, reframe your thinking and change the conversation because you are only strengthening your own self-doubt. Let other people worry about other people's work. Focus on what you were meant to be doing. Jealousy and negative criticism are manifestations of our own insecurities.

Jealousy and negative criticism are manifestations of our own insecurities.

In order to strengthen your belief in yourself, you must continue to do things that cause you to rely on your own abilities and decisions. Increase faith in yourself by staying true to your word and achieving the goals that you set. The more you trust yourself to be capable of achieving your objectives, the more you will persevere.

REFLECTION AND GOAL SETTING

Questions for reflection and goal setting:

1. How important is it to keep your word? Can you think of examples of when you did and when you did not?

2. How often do you negotiate yourself out of doing what you should?

3. How much faith do you have in your ability to accomplish your goals?

4. What do you do when you are feeling angry or resentful?

5. What five goals can you set that will help you build belief in yourself?

6. When is the last time you took a risk? What was it?

7. What are you good at? How much have you improved your skills over the years and in what areas?

CHAPTER FIVE

BUILD THE POWER OF WILL

*"Persistence is an essential factor in the procedure
of transmuting desire into its monetary equivalent.
The basis of persistence is the power of will."*
—NAPOLEON HILL

"Willpower is like a muscle group—it must be exercised."
—WES WATSON

The basis of persistence is the power of will. Willpower, as it is commonly referred to, can also be built with practice. Not only building willpower, but also building the will to do things *well*. Quality matters. Doing tasks wholeheartedly will round out this power of the will even more.

Consider the famous pilot Amelia Earhart's comments:

*"Whether you are flying the Atlantic, selling sausages,
building a skyscraper, driving a truck, or painting
a picture, your greatest power comes from the fact*

that you want tremendously to do that very thing well. And a thing well done usually works out to the benefit of others as well as yourself. This applies to sport, business, and friendship. "

So Ameila Earhart considered the desire to do something well (with excellence and careful attention) to be your greatest power. Think about that for a moment.

Try to be present with each detail of the next task you undertake. Imagine gaining the skill set of doing things well.

Suzanne Evans wrote a book titled, *The Way You Do Anything Is the Way You Do Everything.* The idea behind this statement as a title is evident. Do everything all the way, don't just do enough to get it done, leaving behind quality issues just because you did not care enough. Practice the habit of caring more about the little things you do and that attitude will carry into the bigger things you do and help you to persist and reach your goals.

Again, persistence is about building habits that cause perseverance. Doing things well is one of the habits that strengthens the power of your will and subsequently prepares you to overcome the moments when you want to quit.

Willpower can be built two ways: through restraining yourself or through exercising yourself.

Restraining yourself is when you work on holding back from doing something you want to do like eat a piece of cake when you are trying to lose weight, drinking a beer when you are trying to go 30 days sober or all the way sober, or whatever the impulse might be. Impulse control builds willpower.

Exercising yourself is when you are running a mile, 3 miles, a 5K, whatever—it's pushing your body to do more by using your mind. This is another version of building willpower.

When you have willpower, you really have an ultimate form of confidence. It is not just a mental thing, it is the belief in your body. It is concentration.

Concentrating your energy into one specific area is a powerful channeling force that can be applied to whatever you want.

If you are building a shelf, willpower can be used to help figure out what all needs to be done and to follow the plan until the completion of the project. The same is true for cooking a meal or running a race or filming a video or making a presentation.

That is the beauty of willpower—its versatility. Once you have built this within yourself, there is very little you cannot accomplish. Put it to the test. Work on strengthening your willpower daily through exercise and impulse control. Keep those two things in mind today and do a little bit more tomorrow. The resulting strength will compound, and in a month, two months, and longer you can apply your willpower to different activities in your life and it will surprise you how different those actions feel when you know you have the ability to keep going.

When you have the ability to concentrate for extended periods of time, you will be so much more productive. This is what you are creating for yourself. Willpower alone will be enough to separate you from the pack when it comes to productivity. Build it, use it.

You will see opportunities each day to employ your restraint or force of will. For example, right now, I'd love to get up and go get a drink of water, my back is a little stiff and I have been sitting here for quite some time. However, I know I want to write for another fifteen minutes. Now, I can rationalize getting up and taking one minute to get a drink and walk around the house; I could just add that minute onto my time at the end.

But what is more valuable to me (and you in a similar situation) is to quickly say, "No, I'm going to finish what I started, then as a reward for finishing, I'll get up and go get a drink of water." Talking to yourself like that will keep you working for the amount of time you set for yourself as a goal and builds the willpower and belief in yourself that persistent people have.

So to recap, the following are five steps to increase your willpower:

1. Practice self-discipline and delay gratification.
2. Set clear and specific goals for yourself each day.
3. Practice mindfulness and put in quality work.
4. Keep building and maintaining your healthy habits.
5. Surround yourself with supportive people.

Let's look at each one in more detail:

Practice self-discipline and delay gratification. Self-discipline is the foundation of willpower. Willpower is the foundation of persistence. It's the ability to control your actions and resist temptations. Start small by setting rules for yourself and sticking to them. For example, avoid distractions while working or limit your screen time. With time, self-discipline will become a habit, and your willpower will grow stronger.

Set clear and specific goals for yourself each day. Write down your goals and break them down into smaller, achievable steps. This way, you can track your progress and celebrate each success along the way. Focusing on your goals can provide the necessary motivation to stay on track and resist distractions.

Practice mindfulness and put in quality work. Mindfulness is the practice of being present and fully engaged in the moment. It can improve your self-awareness and increase your willpower. Start by practicing deep breathing, meditation, or prayer. Mindfulness can help you identify and manage triggers that can weaken your willpower, such as stress or fatigue.

Keep building and maintaining your healthy habits. Building healthy habits can increase your willpower. Maintain the staples of your daily routine: exercise, healthy eating, and getting enough sleep. When you take care of your body, your mind will also be sharper, and your willpower will be stronger.

Surround yourself with supportive people (aka the Master Mind). Using your close friends for support can increase your willpower. Avoid people who bring you down or distract you from your goals. Having a supportive network can help you stay on track and resist temptations.

The cool thing about all this is that it is the journey of a lifetime. All of the components of persistence are developed daily and they build upon each other over years to turn your life into something you only imagined when you start.

And you can put as much or as little effort into this skillset as you want. If you push yourself more, you will gain more willpower sooner. It's that simple, what you put in is what you get out as the saying goes. Think about what your ultimate goal is, your dream life, the person you want to become, and use that vision to help you put in more effort.

"Will-power and desire, when properly combined, makes an irresistible pair."—Napoleon Hill

Next we'll talk about how to keep that desire stoked to use as a powerful motivational force throughout your journey to achieving your goals.

REFLECTION AND GOAL SETTING

Questions for reflection and goal setting:

1. How would you describe your current level of willpower?

2. What areas of your life or goals do you find it easy to spend a long time focusing on?

3. What daily tasks do you have a hard time completing?

4. Think about the individuals you would or could consider to be part of your Master Mind group.

5. Do you value quantity or speed over quality? In what areas of your life and goals could you improve your quality of effort?

CHAPTER SIX

FUEL YOUR BURNING DESIRE

"If you find yourself lacking in persistence,
this weakness may be remedied by building
a stronger fire under your desires."

—NAPOLEON HILL, *THINK AND GROW RICH*

Work on becoming single-minded. The name of the game comes down to concentration, and in order to truly concentrate the attention of your thoughts, you must have a focus that is burning hot. A point that is fixed in your mind like a light that can't be extinguished. It has to become a goal that you MUST see come to fruition or be miserable.

To attain that emotion and feeling about your goals, you have to plant those desires so deeply and intensely in yourself that they merge into the subconscious part of your mind. Napoleon Hill teaches how to do this in his classic bestseller, *Think and Grow Rich.*

Consider and test Napoleon Hill's six steps for transforming desire for riches (they work for a different goal, too) into its physical manifestation. With Hill's words in italics, the six steps are:

1. *Fix in your mind the exact amount of money you desire. It is not sufficient merely to say, "I want plenty of money." Be definite as to the amount. (There is a psychological reason for definiteness which will be described in a later chapter.)*

Again, this step applies to whatever your goal is. If you want to achieve a certain promotion or start a specific business or get into better physical condition, whatever your goal—be specific about the details of that desire.

2. *Determine what you intend to give in return for the money you desire. (There is no such thing as something for nothing.)*

What service will you provide? What sacrifices are you willing to make? How much time will you put into attaining your desire? These are all important questions and answers to think about. You may find that your desire does not match what you are willing to do or give in effort or service in return. This is crucial to know the answers early on so you don't waste time on the wrong pursuit.

3. *Establish a definite date when you intend to possess the money you desire.*

You know the importance of putting a date on something you say you are going to accomplish. Make it realistic, but be aggressive. The whole process must have a sense of urgency. Set a date, light a fire under yourself, and don't move the goalposts for when it will be completed.

4. *Create a definite plan for carrying out your desire, and begin at once, whether you are ready or not, to put this plan into action.*

The time to begin this plan is right now. Find some paper, write it down. Start thinking about your plan any chance you get and write down the details. The sooner you get a plan started, the sooner you can start carrying it out. Start today!

5. *Write out a clear, concise statement of the amount of money you intend to acquire, name the time limit for its acquisition, state what you intend to give in return for the money, and describe clearly the plan through which you intend to accumulate it.*

Eventually, it might be helpful to write this on a notecard and keep it with you. But for now write it down here or in the pages in the back of the book. Get it down in writing and begin the process of imprinting this desire and plan into your natural mind.

6. *Read your written statement aloud, twice daily, once just before retiring at night, and once after arising in the morning. AS YOU READ—SEE AND FEEL AND BELIEVE YOURSELF ALREADY IN POSSESSION OF THE MONEY.*

This is how you begin to influence your subconscious and begin to really believe that you can achieve your goal. Stick with this even if it feels weird at first, just do it and keep doing it and see what happens.

Again, this process does not only work in regard to gaining money, but also for any specific goal you wish to accomplish. Try it for six months to start and watch how much more productive and focused you become as your plans and purpose become more concrete and realistic in your mind.

Remember these two steps in the process:

1. Be clear on what it is you want and then being relentless in your pursuit of said wants. It boils down to who quits and who doesn't. Because even if you don't win in the way that you dreamed or imagined—if you don't quit you win anyway. If you quit, you are cursed with all kinds of other weight to walk through life with. Regret. Wondering what might've been. No one needs that.

2. Burn your vision in your mind. Think about it as often as you can and consistently take the steps needed to accomplish your goals. It's natural to get discouraged when the results don't come as quickly as we hope, and then we quit or slow down. This is a mistake. When you feel discouraged, practice doing something that builds you back up.

The quickest way is typically exercise. Whether walking, lifting weights, jogging, or calisthenics, whatever physical work and movement you can get into quickly, go for it. Your mood will improve enough to go back to work. And this is the level of dedication needed to get where you are going by the date you would like to get there. Make sense?

100 REASONS WHY

Successful entrepreneur Stefan James, of Project Life Mastery, recommends writing down 100 reasons why you want to accomplish your ultimate goal, your vision for your life. Once you get 100 reasons written down, you can come back to that list whenever it is needed to give yourself motivation. As you write down the reasons, exaggerate the pleasure of achieving your goals, and also exaggerate the pain you would feel or experience from not having accomplished your goals.

Sacrifice. No one really likes to hear that word, but it works. The more often you are able to forgo satisfying your impulses to quit or indulge in something detrimental to your burning desire, the stronger you become. Your resolution becomes forged in the hardness of repeatedly doing what you NEED to do rather than what you WANT to do.

This tempering is what your character needs to develop to become who you wish to be. Is it pleasant at first? No! That's the point. It's to your advantage to get used to tough situations that you are not accustomed to dealing with in your routine life of desired comforts.

Get out of that rut by introducing some difficulties such as working out, getting up early, not eating every time you want to, not taking cheat days or days off work. I'm not talking about working 24-7, but there has to be an element of grind to your outlook or you'll never achieve your burning desire. Decide today what you want and who you want to be.

The discipline you develop through practicing and perfecting these daily actions and habits will then positively affect your work ethic. Meaning, you will concentrate longer and longer at your work as you will not be succumbing to every temptation for distraction, rest, and relief from pushing yourself to grow.

BE MORE!

All the greatest men are maniacs. They are possessed by a mania which drives them forward towards their goal. The great scientists, the artists, the philosophers, the religious leaders—all maniacs. What else but a blind singleness of purpose could have given focus to their genius, would have kept them in the groove of their purpose? Mania, my dear Mister Bond, is as priceless as genius. Dissipation of energy, fragmentation of vision, loss of momentum, the lack of follow-through—these are the vices of the herd.—Ian Fleming, *Dr. No*

You will gain confidence through this process that cannot be taken away. But most importantly (maybe) is the fact that you will change your mindset to attract the things that you want. In the context of money, Napoleon Hill called this mental awareness, "money conscious." He said:

"Only those who become 'money conscious' ever accumulate great riches. Money consciousness means that the mind has become so thoroughly saturated with the DESIRE for money, that one can see one's self already in possession of it."

As you immerse yourself for longer and longer periods of time in your work, so does your mind dwell longer and longer on the desired results of this work. The action influences the thinking which influences your subconscious to the point where you begin to see yourself as already achieving your burning desire, whatever it might be.

What kind of life do you want to live?

Can you do better than you did yesterday?

Create that hunger that fuels you. You have to feed your burning desire to achieve your goals.

How?

Start physically. Don't give in to your desire to eat right away. We are creatures that for thousands of years probably did not eat every single day. At the very least, we did not live in a constant surplus of food availability which has become commonplace for many today.

We are designed to function while hungry. In fact, we can sometimes function more efficiently when hungry. So pass up that snack for now and get something done while your stomach growls. Drink some water. Let's get some work done!

When you sacrifice repeatedly, you will find that you have accomplished a lot more than you did when you were always satiated and full. I'm not saying to starve yourself, but just to not always grab food just because you crave it or just because you are hungry and it is available.

Make yourself uncomfortable and enjoy the change. You may be surprised how capable and sharp your mind can be in circumstances different from your normal comfortable routines.

The following is a piece that my son shared with me from a poster that was on the wall of one of his classrooms in elementary school. He thought of me and asked the teacher for a copy. Twelve years later, it hangs in front of me in my office while I write. Here's what it reads:

Ready or not, some day it will all come to an end.
There will be no more sunrises, no minutes, or hours or
*   days.*
All the things you collected, whether treasured or forgotten,
*   will pass to someone else.*
Your wealth, fame and temporal power will shrivel to
*   irrelevance.*
It will not matter what you owned or what you were owed.
Your grudges, resentments, frustrations and jealousies will
*   finally disappear.*

So too, your hopes, ambitions, plans and to-do lists will expire.

The wins and losses that once seemed so important will fade away.

It won't matter where you came from or what side of the tracks you lived on at the end.

It won't matter whether you were beautiful or brilliant.

Even your gender and skin color will be irrelevant.

So what will matter? How will the value of your days be measured?

What will matter is not what you bought but what you built,

Not what you got but what you gave.

What will matter is not your success but your significance.

What will matter is not what you learned but what you taught.

What will matter is every act of integrity, compassion, courage or sacrifice that enriched, empowered or encouraged others to emulate your example.

What will matter is note your competence but your character.

What will matter is not how many people you knew, but how many will feel a lasting loss when you're gone.

What will matter is not your memories but the memories of those who loved you.

What will matter is how long you will be remembered,
by whom and for what.

Living a life that matters doesn't happen by accident.
It's not a matter of circumstance but of choice.
Choose to live a life that matters.

—Michael Josephson, *What Will Matter*

Think about what will be said about you after you pass away. What kind of legacy do you want to leave? What are you doing now that would be of lasting impact to other people when you die? Reflecting upon your mortality is a great exercise to help reignite your ambition to achieve the success you imagine.

Then get to work. Another act that fuels ambition is work. The more effort you put in, the more motivated you will get to continue.

"Quantity and persistence will get you the outcomes
you need."—James Altucher

"Quantity and persistence," and I would add consistency. Show up for your loved ones, show up for your followers and anyone else who looks to you for inspiration or motivation. Think about your loved ones. Stop making it about you and make it about being accountable to others—and you will find yourself in a different frame of mind when it comes to doing the work when you don't feel like it.

When you rework your perspective into one of sharing and helping others, your feelings will not matter to you as much.

Other methods for creating that burning desire to continue are positive images of who you will become, images of what you will achieve, and the lifestyle you will be able to live. Find images that represent these things to you and post them prominently as a reminder to you of the future you are working toward.

USE MOMENTUM

In sports like basketball, we hear people talk a lot about momentum. One made or missed shot, an untimely foul, a couple of seconds of time is all it takes to shift the positive momentum from one team to the other. In a close game, whoever has the momentum swinging their way at the end of the game is usually the team who wins the game.

So it is in life. Momentum is something you can create, something that happens through luck, but in any case, you want to take advantage of momentum going your way whenever you can. If you get a sale, if you have a particularly fortuitous turn of events in your life or your side hustle, take the time to double down on your work that day.

If the momentum is driven by a certain marketing campaign or activity that you started, make sure to dive in and focus on learning what is making it work and do more of it. Don't hesitate or bask in your success.

LEARN BY DOING

So many people are overthinking and overlearning. Once you have the basic idea of how to do something, it's time to get out there and do it. You will probably fail at first. At least you will likely not be very good at it right away. Don't be afraid to be seen this way. It's temporary.

You'll learn faster by doing than by listening, watching, or reading. Evaluate yourself right now. What do you want to do that you have researched, watched videos about, read books about, but still have not done much actual work on doing it yourself?

Prioritize one thing on what might be an extensive list, and make that your focus for the week. See what headway you can make by putting into practice all that you know in your mind. Letting yourself ACT and mess up and try again is a big part of keeping the burning desire alive. And who knows, you may have great success on your first attempt, but you'll never know if you just keep learning and learning but not applying what you learn.

Challenge yourself to let go of unrealistic expectations and instead free yourself to try.

Ambition can fluctuate over time, and it's not uncommon to experience a lull in motivation or drive. Reigniting your ambition can be challenging, but here are some other ways to help you get started.

Let go of unrealistic expectations and free yourself to try.

Revisit your goals. Sometimes a lack of ambition can be due to feeling disconnected from your goals. Take some time to reflect on your goals and ask yourself if they still align with your values and aspirations. If not, consider redefining your goals to better support your current vision for your future.

Spend time reflecting on your motivation. Think about what motivates you and why you wanted to achieve your goals in the first place. Reconnecting with your motivation can help reignite your ambition and remind you of the importance of your goals.

Seek inspiration from those who are living a life similar to what you are trying to accomplish. Look for inspiration in the people around you or in the stories of those who have achieved similar goals. Seek out books, podcasts, or other resources that inspire you and help you reconnect with your ambition.

Finally, *taking action is crucial* for reigniting your ambition. Start with small, manageable steps and build momentum over time. Set aside time each day to work toward your goals, even if it's just for a few minutes.

Truth is, you know you don't need to read a book for this information. You know in your heart that what you need to do is put in the work, put in the time and effort, and then do it every single day.

REFLECTION AND GOAL SETTING

Some questions to ask yourself:

1. Have you written out a clear, defined desire as your ultimate goal?

2. What will you do to achieve it?

3. What will you build?

4. Why do you want to achieve this goal?

5. What are some reasons for you personally and who are the people you hope to help by achieving this success?

6. What are you willing to sacrifice?

7. How much time are you willing to put in each day?

8. What do you have going on in your life that may be slowing you down?

9. Are you more motivated by the promise of reward or the threat of punishment?

10. What can you do consistently to increase your ambition?

CHAPTER SEVEN

LIVE WITH GRATITUDE AND ACCOUNTABILITY

Becoming accountable to yourself and others is the final step in gaining persistence as a characteristic of your life. The habit of telling yourself you will achieve a goal and then achieving it is the single most important contributor to your confidence, your faith in yourself and your abilities.

Accountability fueled by faith in yourself will inspire trust and confidence in others.

Daily action as a result of being grateful to have the chance to live up to your potential will take you to level after level of great achievement. All will happen so long as you do not give up. Action is evidence of your gratitude.

Think about what you want to achieve, make your plan to achieve, develop belief in yourself—keeping your vision in mind—and use your abilities and gifts to become what you want to become. Think about WHY you want to achieve your dream. Think of the people you will help, think of the skills and the improvements you will cause within yourself.

On the days you want to quit, this is when you must take control and hold on tight to your vision and only focus on the immediate and important tasks and say no to distractions.

You know you are worthy of this goal. You know you will become good enough to accomplish it. The rest will take care of itself if you take step after step while increasing your belief in yourself. Become different, work harder than the average person unless you are content to be average.

Take action and motivate yourself and be grateful for the chance to be accountable to yourself and others. Let the positive emotions feed on one another and take up so much of your day that there is no room for fear, no room for resentment and self-doubt, there is only room to keep moving forward in an upward direction toward your goals.

Let your gratitude motivate you to action.

ONE-DAY EXPERIMENT

Take a couple of minutes to imagine doing more than you've ever done before in a single day. I'm talking about doing more of the work you know you need to do to accomplish what you want to in life. Imagine just doing for ONE day a level of work that you have NEVER done before. Imagine a measurable goal or goals that you could set for yourself for one day and then pick a day and go for it. Try it.

Imagine how you will feel if you put in a day that you didn't think was even possible in terms of productivity. Imagine you just keep working past when you normally quit just because you want to see how much you could get done if you just didn't quit. ONE DAY. I'm not talking about sustaining 100 hours of work per week. I'm not saying work for 24 hours, but what about 12? What about 14, 16 hours? Have you ever tried it?

Imagine the way it would stretch your mind as to what is actually possible to accomplish in a week, a month, a year.

There is so much potential that we waste without a second thought. That must change if you want to become more than what you are. Start working longer. Get that hunger stimulated and find the gratitude in your work, find the satisfaction of your hunger within the process to improve yourself and reach your goals.

You may have talked negatively to and about yourself for so many years. It is time to reverse the self-talk. It is time to build confidence in yourself through your actions. It is time to earn the trust of others and yourself by following through on the work that you've said you're going to do.

You are not stuck! You will get up and get going because you have done it before. You did it yesterday and the day before and that's how you know you will get it done today.

One day at a time you will prove to yourself what you are made of. You will believe that this is the beginning of a new chapter in your life. Go!

Discipline is the answer you are looking for, not motivation.

Every choice you make brings you closer to your goals or takes you farther away. Think about this throughout the day. You know now that everything you need to know is inside you. All you need is inside in order to take action and to appreciate life, and you will learn the rest through the work.

Stop checking results and trying to use them as motivation. Discipline is the answer you are looking for, not motivation.

MAKE YOURSELF ACCOUNTABLE

Make a pact with yourself. Find someone who will hold you accountable. A group of likeminded individuals, for example. Not all of you have to be trying to achieve the same goal. Maybe one person is trying to start a successful home-based business. Maybe someone else is trying to maintain a diet or exercise program. Someone else might be trying to stop drinking.

Whatever the reasons for motivation, the commonality is that you all need the power of persistence. When you find a partner or someone to check in with daily or weekly, it will help you be true to your conscience and your goals when you know you will be reporting to someone about your success later.

An accountability partner will also offer encouragement and sometimes inspiration.

But again, being accountable to yourself is just as important. Be your own accountability partner who argues with yourself when you want to quit. You have to be ready to flip your negative self-talk to talking positively to and about yourself. You have many good qualities—reinforce your confidence by emphasizing each one each day.

You have to be ready to push yourself when you want to quit on a goal you set for yourself today. Don't try to rationalize not completing the task due to being tired or some unexpected event that put you behind schedule.

Look yourself in the eye in the mirror and tell yourself the truth. Tell yourself your goals. Will you keep your word? Or will you be like so many other people talking, talking, always talking—but finding a reason to quit a few weeks, months, or even years down the road. How long are you willing to put the work in? How will you react if you have to struggle for years before you see results?

You cannot allow yourself to negotiate on what you said you would do. Especially when you said those things to yourself. When you set those goals for yourself today, it is essential that you complete them. If you don't, you will begin to lose faith and confidence in yourself.

REFLECTION AND GOAL SETTING

Plan a day to do more than you've done before on your side hustle or your business or your day job. How much time will you put in that day?

What are you thankful for today?

How can you make yourself more accountable?

What negative self-talk did you allow yourself today and how can you reverse it?

What are three reasons you want to achieve your dream?

CONCLUSION

The whole point of this book is to give you a resource to pick up at any point in your life, any point during your day to give you a boost of confidence. Pick it up and read a page and get a reminder to repeat in your mind to push yourself a little bit longer.

The daily habits you instill will add up to you experiencing the power of persistence. The habits you instill will improve your character and allow you to become the kind of person you need to be to achieve your goals.

Use the power of your mind to envision the person you want to be, the life you want to live, and to exercise the reinforcement through your subconscious mind to change your self-talk into the positive affirmations that will make you believe in yourself.

When you fail, you will learn to use the experience as an opportunity to grow. When you face obstacles and painful circumstances in your life, you will spin them positive and use your newfound belief in yourself to push right through roadblocks.

Throughout your life, you will strengthen the belief and confidence you have in yourself by overcoming adversity. Taking action leads you to faith in your abilities.

Pushing yourself beyond your boundaries physically and mentally builds your willpower. Willpower is the superpower that can be applied to any task that you put your hand or mind to. Willpower makes you stretch the ideas of what you thought was previously possible.

Maybe most importantly, you will live with gratitude and accountability in the forefront of your mind. The gratitude you feel to be alive is shown by the action you take to accomplish your goals. Remember, you are accountable to yourself for setting the goal in the first place. You are accountable to your loved ones and anyone achieving your goals might affect.

The world needs you to accomplish what you set out to do. It all matters.

Taken together, this formula will propel you by the power of persistence and you will no longer be susceptible to self-negotiating. No more quitting. It's the beginning of the rest of your life where you see what is possible if you just keep going with the work you KNOW you should do.

EPILOGUE

From his bestselling book, *Think and Grow Rich*, the following are Napoleon Hill's steps to cultivating persistence and the symptoms of a lack of persistence:

Persistence is a state of mind, therefore it can be cultivated. Like all states of mind, persistence is based upon definite causes, among them these:

a. DEFINITENESS OF PURPOSE. Knowing what one wants is the first and, perhaps, the most important step toward the development of persistence. A strong motive forces one to surmount many difficulties.

b. DESIRE. It is comparatively easy to acquire and to maintain persistence in pursuing the object of intense desire.

c. SELF-RELIANCE. Belief in one's ability to carry out a plan encourages one to follow the plan through with persistence. (Self-reliance can be developed through the principle described in the chapter on auto-suggestion.)

d. DEFINITENESS OF PLANS. Organized plans, even though they may be weak and entirely impractical, encourage persistence.

e. ACCURATE KNOWLEDGE. Knowing that one's plans are sound, based upon experience or observation, encourages persistence; "guessing" instead of "knowing" destroys persistence.

f. CO-OPERATION. Sympathy, understanding, and harmonious cooperation with others tend to develop persistence.

g. WILL-POWER. The habit of concentrating one's thoughts upon the building of plans for the attainment of a definite purpose, leads to persistence.

h. HABIT. Persistence is the direct result of habit. The mind absorbs and becomes a part of the daily experiences upon which it feeds. Fear, the worst of all enemies, can be effectively cured by forced repetition of acts of courage. Everyone who has seen active service in war knows this.

Before leaving the subject of PERSISTENCE, take inventory of yourself, and determine in what particular, if any, you are lacking in this essential quality. Measure yourself courageously, point by point, and see how many of the eight factors of persistence you lack. The analysis may lead to discoveries that will give you a new grip on yourself.

SYMPTOMS OF LACK OF PERSISTENCE:

Here you will find the real enemies which stand between you and noteworthy achievement. Here you will find not only the "symptoms" indicating weakness of PERSISTENCE, but also the deeply seated subconscious causes of this weakness. Study the list carefully, and face yourself squarely IF YOU REALLY WISH TO KNOW WHO YOU ARE, AND WHAT YOU ARE CAPABLE OF DOING. These are the weaknesses which must be mastered by all who accumulate riches:

1. Failure to recognize and to clearly define exactly what one wants.

2. Procrastination, with or without cause. (Usually backed up with a formidable array of alibis and excuses.)

3. Lack of interest in acquiring specialized knowledge.

4. Indecision, the habit of "passing the buck" on all occasions, instead of facing issues squarely. (Also backed by alibis.)

5. The habit of relying upon alibis instead of creating definite plans for the solution of problems.

6. Self-satisfaction. There is but little remedy for this affliction, and no hope for those who suffer from it.

7. Indifference, usually reflected in one's readiness to compromise on all occasions, rather than meet opposition and fight it.

8. The habit of blaming others for one's mistakes, and accepting unfavorable circumstances as being unavoidable.

9. WEAKNESS OF DESIRE, due to neglect in the choice of MOTIVES that impel action.

10. Willingness, even eagerness, to quit at the first sign of defeat. (Based upon one or more of the 6 basic fears.)

11. Lack of ORGANIZED PLANS, placed in writing where they may be analyzed.

12. The habit of neglecting to move on ideas, or to grasp opportunity when it presents itself.

13. WISHING instead of WILLING.

14. The habit of compromising with POVERTY instead of aiming at riches. General absence of ambition to be, to do, and to own.

15. Searching for all the short-cuts to riches, trying to GET without GIVING a fair equivalent, usually reflected in the habit of gambling, endeavoring to drive "sharp" bargains.

16. FEAR OF CRITICISM, failure to create plans and to put them into action, because of what other people will think, do, or say. This enemy belongs at the head of the list, because it generally exists in one's subconscious mind, where its presence is not recognized.

Persistence. Stop quitting on yourself. You've started it, keep going. What else do you want to hear? An easy solution? Magic advice that somehow changes things?

Get to work right now.

How much time do you spend getting it done? There is no easy way. There is no secret formula. Hard work. Long work. Extending the amount of time you spend doing what you know you need to do for your vision of success.

What are you willing to do more of? What are you willing to sacrifice in order to do more of your work? To stay at it longer than you did yesterday?

Even when you are frustrated or uncomfortable or hungry or sad. That is what it will take from you every single day. That's what you will have to give.

Consistency is the magic.

FINAL THOUGHTS

Focus; if you can learn to focus, you will be a persistent person. When you make focus a habit, you will learn the alchemy of being persistent—and you will keep working when tempted by distractions.

Eventually, your habit of focus becomes an attitude through repetition. Your attitude is that of someone who just won't give in. Even though you may fail, even if you backstep and give into temptation, no matter what—your attitude of persistence will nag at you, and you will remember that you have a goal. You will remember what it felt like to not give in, to not give up, and you will want to regain that feeling.

Don't turn away from your dreams just to look at immediately gratifying benefits. Stay with the work just a little longer. Finish what you started and you will never sleep better—and the rewards will be so much more than gratifying.

> *Finish what you started and you will never sleep better.*

Instead of temporary results, become addicted to sticking with it for the long-term satisfaction of reaching your goals and seeing your vision become reality. Become obsessed with not giving in when you want to.

Every time you wander around either physically or mentally, or realize that you're not working, not in a productive flow state, ask yourself, "What am I doing right now?" This moment of self-awareness is often all it takes to re-engage with your work.

And always ask throughout the process if what you are doing, or about to do, will bring you closer to your goals—or not.

"Above all, do not lose your desire to walk. Every day, I walk myself into a state of well-being & walk away from every illness. I have walked myself into my best thoughts, and I know of no thought so burdensome that one cannot walk away from it. But by sitting still, & the more one sits still, the closer one comes to feeling ill. Thus if one just keeps on walking, everything will be all right."—Søren Kierkegaard

ACKNOWLEDGMENTS

Thank you to Eileen Rockwell for the cover design, Angela Shears for editing, Susan Ramundo for the page design, and Christina Lynch and Lisa Ott for managing the printing and distribution of this book.

Thank you for taking the time to read this book! If you found any of this information helpful, please leave a review on the online bookselling platform of your choice.

Additional Recommended Resources

The War of Art by Steven Pressfield

Think and Grow Rich by Napoleon Hill

The Power of Your Subconscious Mind by Joseph Murphy

Unshakable by Jim Rohn

Non-Negotiable by Wes Watson

ABOUT THE AUTHOR

John Martin is a personal development author and content creator dedicated to helping people achieve their full potential. Drawing on years of experience and a deep understanding of the human mindset, he helps individuals—through the use of introspection and self-analysis—identify and overcome internal obstacles that may be holding them back.

John's books, including *Focus on Today*, *Choose Your Perspective*, and *Empower Yourself*, inspire readers to take action and persevere in pursuit of their goals, regardless of their current circumstances. His work has been translated into six languages and has reached a global audience.

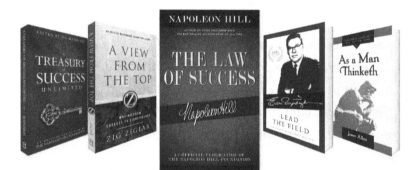